26237

j636.976 Horton-Bussey,
HOR   Claire.

         101 facts about
         ferrets.

$22.60

DATE			
JUN 2 1 2004			
OCT 0 2 2007			

BAKER & TAYLOR

101 FACTS ABOUT

FERRETS

Please visit our web site at: www.garethstevens.com
For a free color catalog describing Gareth Stevens Publishing's
list of high-quality books and multimedia programs,
call 1-800-542-2595 or fax your request to (414) 332-3567.

Library of Congress Cataloging-in-Publication Data

Horton-Bussey, Claire.
   101 facts about ferrets / by Claire Horton-Bussey. — North American ed.
      p. cm. — (101 facts about pets)
   Includes bibliographical references and index.
   Summary: Provides information about ferrets, how to care for them, and how
to understand their behavior.
   ISBN 0-8368-3016-4 (lib. bdg.)
   1. Ferrets as pets—Miscellanea—Juvenile literature. [1. Ferrets as pets.
2. Pets.] I. Title: One hundred one facts about ferrets. II. Title. III. Series.
SF459.F47H67   2002
636.9'76628—dc21   2001049566

This North American edition first published in 2002 by
Gareth Stevens Publishing
A World Almanac Education Group Company
330 West Olive Street, Suite 100
Milwaukee, WI 53212 USA

This U.S. edition © 2002 by Gareth Stevens, Inc. Original edition © 2001 by Ringpress Books
Limited. First published by Ringpress Books Limited, P.O. Box 8, Lydney, Gloucestershire,
GL15 4YN, United Kingdom. Additional end matter © 2002 by Gareth Stevens, Inc.

Ringpress Series Editor: Claire Horton-Bussey
Ringpress Designer: Sara Howell
Gareth Stevens Editors: Jim Mezzanotte and Mary Dykstra

Printed in Hong Kong through Printworks Int. Ltd

2 3 4 5 6 7 8 9 06 05 04 03

101 FACTS ABOUT

FERRETS

Claire Horton-Bussey

Gareth Stevens Publishing
A WORLD ALMANAC EDUCATION GROUP COMPANY

1 Ferrets have lived with humans for thousands of years. Most ferrets are **domesticated** animals.

2 As early as 300 B.C., ancient Romans used ferrets to drive away rats and to find rabbits, which the Romans used for food.

3 Romans took ferrets to other parts of Europe. Later, European travelers brought them to America.

4 In recent times, ferrets have been used to carry cables through tunnels and pipes, in places too small for people to fit.

5 Ferrets can squeeze through small holes because they have flexible ribs. They can flatten their bodies and crawl through the tiniest spaces.

are most closely related to the European polecat.

8 Ferrets can live up to 15 years or more, but most live between six and eight years.

6 Ferrets are not **rodents**, like mice and rats. They are actually similar to dogs and cats.

7 Ferrets belong to the family of animals called **mustelids**. Skunks, weasels, otters, badgers, and polecats are also mustelids. Ferrets

9 Male ferrets are known as hobs, and female ferrets are called jills. Most hobs are larger than jills, and their heads are usually wider and less pointed.

10 When jills reach six months of age, they are usually **neutered**, which means they will not be able to have any babies. If a jill is not neutered, she can get sick and might even die. Very few pet jills have babies.

11 Most hobs are also neutered. When a hob is neutered, he becomes less **aggressive** and does not have as strong an odor.

12 A group of ferrets is called a "business" of ferrets. Ferrets are usually very busy, so this name for a group of them really fits.

15 Ferrets are curious animals that enjoy being around people and playing games. They are not happy all alone in a cage.

13 You could say that a person trying to find something is "ferreting it out." This use of the word "ferret" comes from the way ferrets act when they are hunting.

16 Ferrets love to dig and make tunnels. If pet ferrets are not kept busy with lots of games and toys, they might dig right through carpets and sofas.

14 The word "ferret" comes from the Latin word "furo," which means "thief." Ferrets are good at taking and hiding things – just like thieves!

17 If you want to own a pet ferret, first ask a **veterinarian**, or animal doctor, if you can keep a ferret where you live. Some towns and cities do not allow people to keep ferrets.

18 In some towns and cities, you will need a special permit before you can buy and keep a ferret.

19 You need to find a **breeder** in order to buy a ferret. A breeder raises and sells ferrets.

20 A baby ferret is called a kit, and a group of kits is called a **litter**.

21 A jill carries her babies in her body for 40 to 44 days before they are born.

22 The average litter of ferrets contains between six and eight kits. A jill can have up to four litters a year, but having that many babies would be very bad for her health.

25 At ten days of age, a kit gets its **milk teeth**, which are its first set of teeth. A kit's canine teeth, which are long, sharp teeth at the sides of its mouth, appear after about six weeks.

23 When kits are first born, they cannot see or hear. Because they have very little fur on their bodies, they need their mother and each other to stay warm.

26 When a kit is 10 to 12 weeks old, it is ready to leave the litter for a new home.

24 After about five days, a kit's fur starts to grow and cover its body. A young ferret's eyes and ears start working about three weeks after it is born.

27 When you select a kit, remember that a healthy kit should be lively and curious. Its coat should be clean and soft. Its nose and ears should be clean, too, and its eyes should look bright.

28 Before choosing a kit for a pet, ask the breeder to handle the kits to see how they behave. An aggressive or nervous kit may not be used to much human contact. Choose a kit that seems to like people, instead of one that seems to fear them.

29 Ferrets come in lots of different colors. When you pick out a kit, you will have to decide which color you like best.

30 An **albino** ferret (above) has white fur and red eyes. Albino ferrets are different from ordinary white ferrets, which have dark eyes.

31 A sable ferret (below) has a top layer of dark brown fur and darker feet. Its **undercoat**, or bottom layer of fur, is lighter.

32 Some ferrets have a top layer of fur that is the same color as a chocolate bar, and an undercoat that is a lighter shade of brown.

33 A cinnamon ferret (above) has fur that is reddish brown and legs that are a darker color.

34 The fur of Siamese ferrets is a lighter color on their bodies than on their legs and tails – just like Siamese cats.

11

37 Ferrets with lighter colors on their feet are said to have mitts, even though they look like they are wearing socks. A ferret with lighter colors on its legs is said to have stockings.

35 A ferret can have patterns on its coat, too. Dalmatian ferrets have dark spots on a white coat, just like dalmatian dogs.

38 Some ferrets have a blaze, which is a white stripe that runs from the forehead down the neck.

36 Some ferrets have a mask (above), which is coloring on the face that makes a ferret look like it is wearing a mask — just like a bandit!

39 A ferret with a bib (opposite, above) has white coloring on its chest, so it looks like it is wearing a baby's bib.

In winter, a ferret grows more of an undercoat so it can stay warm. Its undercoat is a lighter color than its top layer of fur.

42 Because a ferret by itself easily becomes bored, you might want to get two kits instead of one. If you have two kits, they can play with each other when you cannot be with them.

40 As a ferret grows older, its colors get lighter. Ferrets can have gray or white hairs when they are very old, just like people.

41 Ferrets often look lighter in winter than they do in summer.

43 Although some ferrets live outdoors, a pet ferret should be kept inside, so it does not become bored and lonely. A ferret will be happier with people around, and indoor ferrets usually have more contact with people.

44 Before you bring a ferret home, make sure your house is safe.

Check for any holes that it could use to escape, and make sure there are no harmful plants or electrical wires that it might chew on.

45 If you have small pets, such as mice, hamsters, or gerbils, keep them in a separate room, away from your ferret. The door to this room should be kept closed so your ferret cannot sneak inside.

46 A ferret usually gets along well with dogs and cats. They often become playmates. Do not, however,

leave a ferret alone with a dog or cat, and be careful when the animals meet for the first time. They should get used to each other gradually.

47 You should provide your ferret with a roomy cage, where it will be safe and comfortable when it is sleeping. Ferrets have been known to sleep 15 to 20 hours a day!

48 Never keep your ferret in its cage all day long. It will become very unhappy! Ferrets need time to play and exercise. Make sure your ferret spends at least two hours a day outside its cage.

49 Line the bottom of your ferret's cage with shredded paper. Then add a little box that has a towel inside for a bed, and your ferret will have a cozy place to sleep.

50 A ferret's cage needs to be strong and sturdy. A wooden box with wire mesh across the front makes an ideal cage.

51 Always keep the cage door closed when your ferret is inside. Be sure the cage has a solid floor, so your pet cannot dig through the bottom.

52 Place your ferret's cage out of direct sunlight and chilly drafts, so your pet does not get too hot or too cold.

53 Give your pet fresh water every day, in a clean water bottle. Make sure to use a heavy food bowl that will not tip over when your ferret is eating.

food bowl

bedding material

play toy

litter box

shop should have a special dry ferret food that you can buy. If you cannot find ferret food, give your ferret a high-quality dry cat food.

56 A ferret is a meat-eater, or **carnivore**. Although ferrets mostly eat meat, they also enjoy snacks of raw fruits and vegetables.

54 Wash your ferret's food dish every day. You should also make sure that your pet can always get to its water bottle.

55 You should feed your pet several small meals a day, instead of one big meal. Your local pet

57 Get to know your pet's appetite so you can feed it the right amount. A package of ferret food has instructions telling you how much to feed your ferret, but all ferrets are different.

58 Being overweight is very bad for a ferret's health. You should always be able to feel the ribs along your ferret's chest,

but, remember, a ferret should not look too skinny.

59 For an occasional treat, your ferret can eat a raw egg – which it will love! Do not, however, feed a ferret more than one egg a week. A ferret that eats too many eggs might become bald. Never feed your pet chocolate or sugary foods.

60 Pet ferrets are easily housebroken. Fill a litter box with 1½ inches (4 centimeters) of cat litter. Put it in a corner of the room where you keep your ferret.

61 Your ferret will need to use the litter box when it wakes up, after it has been playing, and after it has eaten. Make sure you place your ferret in the litter box at these times.

62 Ask an adult to help you empty the litter box every day. Ferrets are very clean, so your pet will not like using a dirty litter box.

63 The first few times your ferret uses its litter box, reward it with a tasty treat. Ferrets need to know that using a litter box is good behavior.

65 Handle your ferret firmly but gently. When you pick it up, place one hand over its shoulders, with your fingers wrapped around the front of its chest. Support the animal's lower body with your other hand. Your ferret should be very comfortable in this position.

66 You should never pick up a ferret that is half asleep, because it might get scared and **nip**, or bite, you. Ferrets are very deep sleepers, and they need a little time to wake up and be fully alert.

64 Ferrets should be handled a lot when they are kits, so they will be comfortable with people. An adult should help you when you first handle a kit.

69 To teach your ferret to come to you, call its name, then show it a tasty treat. Your pet will learn that when you call, it should come right away!

67 Ferrets nip a lot when they are kits, but you can teach your ferret that nipping is not allowed.

68 If your ferret nips you, say "no" with a firm voice and then ignore the animal, so it learns that nipping people is bad and is not part of a game.

72 You should practice walking your ferret on a leash indoors. Before you take a ferret outside, it needs **vaccinations**.

73 After taking a few steps forward, call your pet's name and offer it a treat, so it will follow you.

70 A ferret can also be trained to walk on a leash. You need to buy a harness that fits over your pet's body. Pet stores usually have harnesses.

71 First, your ferret has to get comfortable wearing just its harness. Then you can attach a leash.

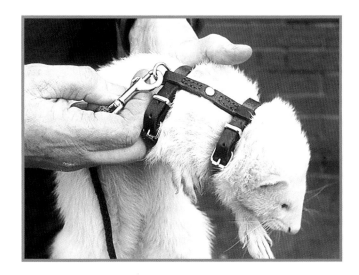

22

76 Ferrets are full of energy. You should play with your ferret several times a day.

77 A ferret will have hours of fun with golf balls, plastic pipes, and cardboard tubes.

74 You can even train a ferret to climb over boxes or through hoops. Hold a treat in your hand and the ferret will follow it.

75 By holding a treat up high, you can also train a ferret to stand on its back legs.

80 In nice weather, your ferret can play outside in an enclosed area. Just make sure it cannot dig a hole and escape!

81 Always keep your ferret in a shaded area when it is outside, and make sure it has water.

78 Try hiding from your ferret and calling its name. When your pet finds you, give it a treat.

79 Using sturdy boxes, create a maze of tunnels for your ferret to explore. Ferrets also enjoy playing in pillowcases and sleeping bags!

82 Like skunks and other mustelids, ferrets have a strong scent.

They release this scent when they feel threatened.

83 A ferret also uses its scent to warn other animals to stay away from its territory.

84 To keep your house from having a bad odor, change the bedding in your ferret's cage every day.

85 A ferret has a very thick coat of fur. The stiff top layer is waterproof, while the undercoat is much softer and helps keep the animal warm.

86 To **groom** a ferret, use a brush with medium-soft bristles. You should also comb a ferret's hair to remove any tangles.

87 Every spring and fall, your ferret will **molt**, or shed its coat of fur. A new coat soon grows back.

88 If you wash a ferret too often, it loses the natural oils in its coat. It then produces even more oil and becomes smellier than before! A bath every few months, using ferret or cat shampoo, is enough.

89 If your ferret gets fleas, you should wash its coat with a kitten-safe flea shampoo. Be sure to rinse your ferret's coat thoroughly, then dry it with a towel.

90 If your ferret's nails do not wear down naturally, you might have to cut them. Ask a veterinarian how to trim a ferret's nails.

26

91 Feeding your ferret a hard, dry food should help keep its teeth clean. If you think your pet's teeth need cleaning, ask a veterinarian for help.

92 Check your ferret's ears regularly. They should look clean and smell

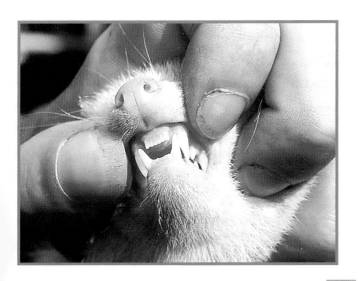

fresh. If you see a dark gray wax and smell a bad odor, talk to a veterinarian. Your pet may have ear **mites**.

93 Every year, your ferret should see a veterinarian for a general check-up and vaccinations to help it stay healthy.

95 When a ferret is very frightened or is in pain, it screams.

96 Like a cat, a ferret will hiss when it is fighting. By hissing, a ferret lets other animals know that it is very angry and should be left alone.

97 When a ferret feels threatened, it may fluff up its tail to look bigger and more dangerous.

94 Ferrets make a lot of interesting noises. A ferret whines if it is excited and makes a giggling or chuckling sound when it is playing and having fun.

100 If your ferret sneezes, it may have a cold. Always talk to a veterinarian if you think your ferret might be sick.

101 As long as you care for a ferret properly, it will give you a lot of love and be a fun pet for many years to come.

98 A ferret may try to trick other animals into thinking it is bigger and stronger than it actually is by making all of its hair stand on end.

99 When ferrets are nervous or excited, they sometimes shiver.

29

Glossary

aggressive: to act forceful or seem ready to attack.

albino: an animal or person whose skin, hair, and eyes lack color.

breeder: a person who raises and sells a certain kind of animal.

carnivore: a meat-eating animal.

domesticated: not wild, and comfortable living with humans.

groom: to brush or clean an animal's coat so it looks nice.

litter: a group of baby animals born at the same time to the same mother.

milk teeth: a mammal's first teeth

mites: tiny insects that live and feed on a plant or an animal.

molt: to shed a coat of fur before growing a new one.

mustelids: a group of mammals, including ferrets, polecats, otters, and weasels, that are carniverous and produce a powerful scent.

neutered: given an operation that makes it impossible to produce any young.

nip: to bite quickly and lightly.

rodents: a group of animals, including hamsters, rats, mice, and gerbils, that gnaw with their front teeth.

undercoat: the soft bottom layer of fur on a ferret's coat.

vaccinations: injections, or shots, that keep people and animals from getting sick.

veterinarian: a doctor whose job is making sure that animals stay healthy.

More Books to Read

All About Your Ferret
Sheila Crompton
(Barrons)

Ferrets (Naturebooks series)
Mary Berendes
(Childs World)

Ferrets (Nature Watch series)
Sylvia A. Johnson
(Carolrhoda Books)

My Pet Ferrets (All About Pets series) Amy Gelman
(Lerner)

Web Sites

Ferret Central
www.ferretcentral.org/

Grin and Ferret
http://homearts.com/depts/
pastime/37ferrf1.htm

The Ferret House
www.theferrethouse.com

The Ferret Nook: Ferret Care
www.ferretnook.com/
ferretcare.html

To find additional web sites, use a reliable search engine, such as www.yahooligans.com, with one or more of the following keywords: **ferret, ferret care, pet ferrets, mustelids.**

Index